Financial Education for Teenagers: A Step-by-Step Guide

"Money Matters: A Teen's Guide to Financial Education"

Charles Augustus Tegart

Table of Contents

1. Introduction
2. Chapter 1: *Understanding Money*
3. Chapter 2: *The Basics of Personal Finance and Why Financial Education is Essential for Teenagers*
4. Chapter 3: *Financial Independence for Teenagers*
5. Chapter 4: *Budgeting Basics*
6. Chapter 5: *Saving Money*
7. Chapter 6: *Smart Spending*
8. Chapter 7: *Understanding Credit and Debt*
9. Chapter 8: *Introduction to Investing*
10. Chapter 9: *Setting and Achieving Financial Goals*
11. Chapter 10: *Earning Money*
12. Chapter 11: *Understanding Taxes*
13. Chapter 12: *Protecting Your Finances*
14. Chapter 13: *Financial Tools and Resources*
15. Chapter 14: *The Importance of Philanthropy*
16. Conclusion
17. Glossary
18. Resources for Further Learning

Introduction

Welcome to **"Money Matters: A Teen's Guide to Financial Education"**! This book is designed to help you navigate the world of personal finance and build a strong foundation for managing your money effectively. Whether you're saving for college, planning for your future, or simply trying to make sense of your finances, this guide will provide you with the knowledge and tools you need to succeed.

As a teenager, you have a unique opportunity to learn about money management and develop good financial habits early on. By understanding key concepts like budgeting, saving, investing, and protecting your finances, you can take control of your financial future and make informed decisions that will benefit you for years to come.

Throughout this book, you'll learn practical strategies for managing your money, setting financial goals, and making smart financial decisions. From creating a budget and saving for your goals to understanding taxes and investing for the future, each chapter will cover essential topics to help you build financial literacy and confidence.

Whether you're earning money from a part-time job, planning for college, or thinking about your long-term goals, this book will provide you with the knowledge and skills you need to succeed. By taking an active role in your financial education, you can set yourself up for success and achieve your dreams.

So let's dive in and explore the world of personal finance together. Whether you're a beginner or already have some experience with managing money, there's always something new to learn. Get ready to take charge of your finances and make your money work for you!

Let's get started on this exciting journey towards financial empowerment and independence!

Chapter 1: Understanding Money

What is Money?

Money is something we use every day, but do we really understand what it is? At its core, money is a tool that facilitates the exchange of goods and services. Imagine trying to trade your phone for a pair of shoes. It would be complicated and time-consuming to find someone who has the shoes you want and also wants your phone. Money solves this problem by acting as a common medium of exchange that everyone values.

The Forms of Money

Money comes in various forms:

- **Cash:** Physical currency like coins and paper bills.
- **Digital Currency:** Money stored and exchanged electronically, like in bank accounts or mobile payment apps.
- **Cryptocurrency:** A type of digital or virtual currency that uses cryptography for security, such as Bitcoin.

The Role of Money

Money has three main roles in our lives:

1. Medium of Exchange: Money makes it easy to trade goods and services without the complications of bartering.
2. Store of Value: Money can be saved and retrieved in the future, retaining its value over time.
3. Unit of Account: Money provides a standard measure of value, making it easy to compare the worth of different goods and services.

Why is Money Important?

Understanding the importance of money is the first step toward managing it effectively. Money allows you to:

- **Buy Essentials:** Purchase necessary items like food, clothing, and shelter.
- **Save for the Future:** Set aside money for future needs or goals.
- **Invest:** Grow your wealth by investing in opportunities that yield returns.
- **Handle Emergencies:** Have a financial safety net for unexpected expenses.

Key Terms to Know

- **Income:** Money you earn or receive, such as from a job, allowance, or gifts.
- **Expenses:** Money you spend on goods and services.
- **Savings:** Money you set aside for future use.
- **Budget:** A plan for how you will spend and save your money.
- **Credit:** The ability to borrow money with the promise to repay it.
- **Debt:** Money you owe to others.

Activity: Track Your Money

To better understand your financial habits, start by tracking your money for one month. Write down every source of income and every expense, no matter how small. At the end of the month, review your list to see where your money is coming from and where it's going. This activity will help you become more aware of your financial behavior and identify areas where you can improve.

Summary

Money is an essential tool in our lives that helps us buy goods and services, save for the future, and invest in opportunities. By understanding what money is and why it's important, you can begin to manage your finances more effectively.

Chapter 2: The Basics of Personal Finance and Why Financial Education is Essential for Teenagers

Introduction to Personal Finance

Personal finance refers to the management of your individual or household finances. It involves understanding how to budget, save, invest, and manage money effectively to achieve your financial goals. Developing a strong foundation in personal finance is essential for making informed financial decisions and building a secure financial future.

Why Financial Education is Essential for Teenagers

Financial education equips you with the knowledge and skills needed to navigate the complex world of money management. Here's why it's crucial for teenagers:

1. Early Start: Learning about personal finance early on sets the stage for lifelong financial habits. The sooner you start, the more time you have to build wealth and secure your financial future.

2. Avoiding Debt: Understanding how to manage money helps you avoid unnecessary debt and the stress that comes with it. You'll learn to live within your means and make informed borrowing decisions.

3. Financial Independence: Financial education empowers you to take control of your finances and work towards financial independence. You'll be better equipped to make decisions that align with your goals and values.

4. Informed Decisions: With a solid financial education, you can make informed choices about spending, saving, investing, and planning for the future. This helps you avoid common financial pitfalls and achieve your goals more effectively.

5. Building Wealth: Knowledge of investing and saving strategies enables you to grow your wealth over time. You'll learn how to leverage opportunities for long-term financial growth.

Key Concepts of Personal Finance

1. Budgeting

Budgeting is the process of creating a plan for how you will spend your money. A budget helps you track your income and expenses, ensuring that you live within your means and allocate money towards your financial goals. Key components of budgeting include:

- **Income:** Money you receive from jobs, allowances, gifts, or other sources.
- **Expenses:** Money you spend on needs (e.g., food, rent, transportation) and wants (e.g., entertainment, hobbies).
- **Savings:** Money set aside for future goals, emergencies, or investments.

2. Saving

Saving involves setting aside a portion of your income for future use. Savings can help you achieve short-term goals (e.g., buying a new phone) and long-term goals (e.g., college tuition, buying a car). Important aspects of saving include:

- **Emergency Fund:** A savings buffer for unexpected expenses, such as medical bills or car repairs.
- **Interest:** Earnings on your savings, which can grow over time through compound interest.

3. Investing

Investing is the act of putting money into financial assets (e.g., stocks, bonds, mutual funds) with the expectation of earning a return. Investing helps you grow your wealth over time and achieve long-term financial goals. Key points to understand about investing include:

- **Risk and Return:** Higher potential returns often come with higher risks.
- **Diversification:** Spreading investments across different assets to reduce risk.
- **Time Horizon:** The length of time you plan to hold an investment, which influences your investment choices.

4. Managing Debt

Managing debt involves borrowing money responsibly and paying it back on time. It's important to understand the types of debt (e.g., student loans, credit card debt) and how to manage them effectively. Key considerations include:

- **Interest Rates:** The cost of borrowing money, which can vary based on the type of loan.
- **Repayment Plans:** Strategies for paying off debt, including prioritizing high-interest debt and making consistent payments.

5. Financial Planning

Financial planning involves setting financial goals and creating a plan to achieve them. This includes budgeting, saving, investing, and managing debt. Effective financial planning helps you make strategic decisions that align with your long-term objectives.

Practical Steps to Enhance Financial Education

1. Read Books and Articles: Expand your knowledge by reading books and articles on personal finance. Look for reputable sources and authors with expertise in the field.

2. Take Online Courses: Enroll in online courses or attend workshops on personal finance. Platforms like Coursera, Udemy, and Khan Academy offer accessible and affordable options.

3. Use Financial Apps: Leverage financial apps like Mint, YNAB (You Need a Budget), and Acorns to manage your budget, track expenses, and start investing.

4. Seek Mentorship: Find mentors, such as parents, teachers, or financial advisors, who can provide guidance and support as you navigate your financial journey.

5. Practice: Apply what you learn by creating a budget, setting savings goals, and exploring investment opportunities. Practice helps reinforce your knowledge and build confidence.

Summary

Understanding the basics of personal finance and the importance of financial education is crucial for teenagers. By learning how to manage money effectively, you can avoid common financial pitfalls, achieve your goals, and build a secure financial future. Remember, financial education is a lifelong journey. Stay curious, keep learning, and take control of your financial destiny. In the next chapter, we'll explore the concept of financial independence and how to achieve it as a teenager.

Chapter 3: Financial Independence for Teenagers

Understanding Financial Independence

Financial independence is the ability to support yourself financially without relying on others for money or assistance. It means having enough income and resources to cover your expenses, achieve your goals, and live the life you want without being financially dependent on parents, guardians, or others.

Why Financial Independence Matters

Achieving financial independence offers numerous benefits and opportunities:

- **Freedom:** Financial independence gives you the freedom to make choices based on your own priorities and values, rather than being limited by financial constraints.
- **Security:** Financial independence provides a safety net in case of unexpected expenses, job loss, or economic downturns, giving you peace of mind and security.
- **Opportunities:** Financial independence opens up opportunities for personal and professional growth, allowing you to pursue your passions, interests, and goals without financial constraints.
- **Empowerment:** Financial independence empowers you to take control of your financial future, make informed decisions, and build wealth over time.

How to Achieve Financial Independence as a Teenager

While achieving complete financial independence may not be feasible during your teenage years, there are steps you can take to work towards financial independence and build a solid foundation for your future:

1. Understand Financial Basics

Educate yourself about basic financial concepts such as budgeting, saving, investing, and managing debt. Develop good money habits early on to lay the groundwork for financial independence.

2. Earn Money

Start earning money through part-time jobs, freelancing, or entrepreneurial ventures. Use your earnings to cover your expenses, save for the future, and invest in your goals.

3. Save and Invest Wisely

Save a portion of your income regularly and invest it wisely to grow your wealth over time. Take advantage of compound interest and long-term investment strategies to maximize your returns.

4. Avoid Debt

Be cautious about taking on debt, especially high-interest debt like credit card debt. Avoid unnecessary borrowing and focus on living within your means to avoid financial strain in the future.

5. Set Financial Goals

Define your financial goals and create a plan to achieve them. Whether it's saving for college, starting a business, or buying a home, having clear goals gives you direction and motivation to work towards financial independence.

6. Build Marketable Skills

Invest in developing skills and expertise that are in demand in the job market. Building marketable skills increases your earning potential and opens up opportunities for career advancement and financial success.

7. Be Resourceful

Learn to be resourceful and find creative ways to save money, earn extra income, and make the most of your resources. Look for opportunities to reduce expenses, find affordable alternatives, and leverage your skills and talents.

8. Seek Guidance

Don't be afraid to seek guidance and advice from parents, teachers, mentors, or financial professionals. Learning from others' experiences and expertise can help you make informed decisions and avoid common pitfalls on your path to financial independence.

Summary

While achieving financial independence as a teenager may seem daunting, it's possible to take steps towards building a secure financial future. By understanding financial basics, earning money, saving and investing wisely, setting goals, and seeking guidance, you can work towards financial independence and create the life you envision for yourself. Remember, financial independence is a journey, not a destination. Start early, stay disciplined, and stay focused on your goals, and you'll be well on your way to achieving financial independence and building a brighter future for yourself. In the next chapter, we'll dive deeper into the importance of budgeting and how to create a budget that works for you as a teenager.

Chapter 4: Budgeting Basics

What is a Budget?

A budget is a plan for how you will use your money. It helps you track your income (money coming in) and expenses (money going out) to ensure you are living within your means. Creating a budget is the foundation of good money management because it allows you to see where your money is going and make informed decisions about how to use it.

Why Budgeting is Important

Budgeting is essential because it helps you:

- **Control Your Spending:** Avoid overspending by knowing your limits.
- **Save for the Future:** Allocate money towards savings goals like college, a car, or a new phone.
- **Prepare for Emergencies:** Set aside money for unexpected expenses.
- **Reduce Stress:** Knowing that you have a plan for your money can give you peace of mind.

Steps to Create a Budget

Creating a budget might seem daunting, but it's easier than you think. Here's a step-by-step guide to help you get started:

1. List Your Income

Start by listing all the sources of your income. This could include:

- **Allowance:** Money given to you by your parents or guardians.
- **Part-Time Job:** Earnings from a job you have after school or on weekends.
- **Gifts:** Money received from birthdays, holidays, or special occasions.

2. List Your Expenses

Next, write down all your expenses. It's helpful to categorize them into two groups:

- **Needs (Essentials):** These are things you must have or pay for, such as:
    - Food
    - School supplies
    - Transportation
    - Savings

- **Wants (Non-Essentials):** These are things you would like to have but don't necessarily need, such as:
    - Entertainment (movies, video games)
    - Eating out
    - New clothes
    - Hobbies

3. Track Your Spending

For a month, keep a record of everything you spend. This will give you a clear picture of your spending habits. You can use a notebook, a spreadsheet, or a budgeting app to keep track.

4. Compare Income and Expenses

At the end of the month, compare your total income to your total expenses. This will help you see if you are living within your means. If your expenses are higher than your income, you need to find ways to cut back.

5. Adjust as Needed

Based on your comparison, make adjustments to your spending. Look for areas where you can reduce expenses. For example, if you're spending a lot on eating out, consider cooking more at home.

Budgeting Tips

- **Use a Budgeting App:** Apps like Mint, YNAB (You Need A Budget), or PocketGuard can help you keep track of your income and expenses easily.
- **Review Regularly:** Check your budget at least once a month to see if you need to make any adjustments.
- **Set Realistic Goals:** Make sure your budget reflects your actual income and expenses. Don't set unrealistic expectations that you can't meet.
- **Include Savings:** Treat savings as an essential expense. Aim to save a portion of your income each month.

Example Budget

Here's an example of what a simple monthly budget might look like:

Category	Income	Expenses
Income		
Allowance	$50	
Part-Time Job	$200	
Total Income	**$250**	
Expenses		
Food		$40
School Supplies		$20
Transportation		$30
Entertainment		$30
Savings		$60
Total Expenses		**$180**
Balance		**$70**

In this example, the total income is $250 and the total expenses are $180, leaving a balance of $70. This remaining amount can be added to savings or used for future expenses.

Activity: Create Your Own Budget

Now that you understand the basics of budgeting, it's time to create your own budget. Use the steps and tips provided to list your income and expenses. Track your spending for a month and make adjustments as needed. This practice will help you develop good financial habits and ensure you're on the right path to achieving your financial goals.

Summary

Budgeting is a crucial skill for managing your money wisely. By creating a budget, you can control your spending, save for the future, prepare for emergencies, and reduce financial stress. Remember to review and adjust your budget regularly to stay on track. In the next chapter, we'll explore the importance of saving money and how to do it effectively.

Chapter 5: Saving Money

Why Save Money?

Saving money is crucial for financial stability and future planning. It provides a safety net for emergencies, enables you to reach your financial goals, and gives you the freedom to make important life choices. Learning to save early helps you develop good habits that will benefit you throughout your life.

The Benefits of Saving

1. Emergency Fund: Life is unpredictable. Having money saved can help you cover unexpected expenses like medical bills, car repairs, or sudden travel needs without stress.
2. Future Goals: Whether you want to buy a new phone, save for college, or plan a trip, saving helps you achieve these goals.
3. Financial Security: Savings provide a cushion that can help you feel more secure about your financial future.
4. Earning Interest: Money saved in a bank account can earn interest, which means your savings grow over time.

How to Start Saving

Starting to save money doesn't have to be difficult. Here are some steps to get you started:

1. Set a Savings Goal

Decide what you're saving for and how much money you need. Having a clear goal will motivate you to save. For example, if you want to buy a new laptop that costs $600, your goal is to save $600.

2. Open a Savings Account

Opening a savings account is a safe and effective way to store your money. Choose a bank that offers good interest rates and no monthly fees for teenagers. Having a savings account helps you keep your money safe and separate from your spending money.

3. Save Regularly

Make saving a habit by setting aside a portion of your income each time you receive money. Aim to save a specific percentage of your income, like 10% or 20%. If you earn $100 a month from a part-time job, saving 20% means you set aside $20 each month.

4. Automate Your Savings

Many banks offer the option to set up automatic transfers from your checking account to your savings account. Automating your savings ensures that you consistently save money without having to think about it.

Saving Strategies

Here are some practical strategies to help you save more effectively:

1. Pay Yourself First

Treat your savings like an essential expense. When you receive money, set aside your savings first before spending on anything else.

2. Avoid Impulse Purchases

Impulse purchases can quickly deplete your savings. Before buying something, ask yourself if it's a need or a want. Give yourself time to think about the purchase. If you still want it after a few days, then consider buying it.

3. Look for Discounts and Deals

Be a smart shopper by looking for discounts, coupons, and sales. This way, you can save money on the things you need to buy and have more left over to save.

4. Save Windfalls

Whenever you receive unexpected money, such as birthday gifts or bonuses, save a significant portion of it. It's tempting to spend windfalls, but saving them can boost your savings significantly.

The Power of Compound Interest

One of the most powerful benefits of saving money in a bank account is earning interest. Compound interest is when you earn interest on both the money you've saved and the interest that money earns. Over time, this can significantly increase your savings.

Example of Compound Interest

Imagine you save $500 in a bank account that earns 5% interest per year. After the first year, you'll have $525 ($500 + $25 interest). In the second year, you'll earn interest on $525, giving you $551.25 at the end of the second year. The interest you earn each year increases as your savings grow, thanks to compound interest.

Activity: Start a Savings Challenge

To make saving fun, start a savings challenge. Here are a couple of ideas:

- **52-Week Challenge:** Save a small amount of money in the first week and increase the amount each week. For example, save $1 in the first week, $2 in the second week, and so on. By the end of 52 weeks, you'll have saved $1,378.
- **No-Spend Challenge:** Choose a day, week, or month where you avoid spending money on non-essential items. Save the money you would have spent.

Summary

Saving money is a key aspect of financial health and security. It helps you prepare for emergencies, achieve your goals, and build a solid financial foundation. By setting savings goals, opening a savings account, and using smart saving strategies, you can develop a habit of saving that will benefit you for years to come. In the next chapter, we'll discuss how to spend money wisely and make informed financial decisions.

Chapter 6: Smart Spending

Making Wise Spending Choices

Smart spending is about making informed decisions on how to use your money. It's not about never spending but rather about spending thoughtfully and purposefully. By being a smart spender, you can enjoy your money today while still saving for the future.

The Importance of Smart Spending

Smart spending helps you:

- **Stay Within Your Budget:** Avoid overspending and stay on track with your financial plan.
- **Maximize Value:** Get the most out of your money by choosing quality over quantity.
- **Achieve Financial Goals:** Save more for future goals by reducing unnecessary expenses.
- **Avoid Debt:** Prevent accumulating debt by spending within your means.

Tips for Smart Spending

1. Prioritize Needs Over Wants

Always ensure that your essential needs are met before spending money on non-essential wants. Needs include items like food, clothing, school supplies, and transportation. Wants are things like the latest video game, eating out, or concert tickets.

2. Create a Shopping List

Before you go shopping, make a list of what you need. Stick to this list to avoid impulse buys. This helps you stay focused on what's necessary and prevents you from buying things you don't need.

3. Do Your Research

Before making a purchase, especially for more expensive items, do some research:

- **Compare Prices:** Check prices at different stores and online to find the best deal.
- **Read Reviews:** Look at reviews to ensure the product meets your needs and is of good quality.
- **Wait for Sales:** If it's not urgent, wait for sales or discounts to get a better price.

4. Avoid Impulse Buys

Impulse buys can quickly drain your money. Before buying something on a whim, give yourself some time to think about it. Ask yourself if you really need it and if it fits into your budget. Often, you'll find that you don't really need the item after some reflection.

5. Use Cash Instead of Cards

Using cash can help you stick to your budget because it makes spending feel more real. When you use a card, it's easier to overspend since you don't physically see the money leaving your wallet.

6. Take Advantage of Discounts and Deals

Look for ways to save money on your purchases:

- **Coupons:** Use coupons from newspapers, websites, or apps.
- **Student Discounts:** Many stores and services offer discounts for students.
- **Loyalty Programs:** Join store loyalty programs to earn rewards and save money.

Questions to Ask Before Buying

To make wise spending choices, ask yourself the following questions before making a purchase:

1. Do I really need this?
2. Can I afford it?
3. Is there a better deal available?
4. Will I use it often?
5. Can I wait for a sale?

The Benefits of Delayed Gratification

Delayed gratification means resisting the temptation to make an immediate purchase and waiting for a later reward. This skill can help you make better financial decisions and achieve your long-term goals. For example, instead of buying a new gadget right away, save that money and wait until you have enough to buy something even more meaningful or useful.

Budgeting for Fun

It's important to enjoy your money, too. Budgeting for fun allows you to spend on things you enjoy without guilt. Set aside a portion of your budget specifically for entertainment or hobbies. This way, you can enjoy your spending while still staying within your financial limits.

Activity: Create a Spending Plan

Create a spending plan for your next month. List out your anticipated income and necessary expenses, then allocate some money for savings and fun spending. Track your actual spending throughout the month and compare it to your plan. This activity will help you become more aware of your spending habits and make adjustments where necessary.

Summary

Smart spending is about making informed and thoughtful decisions with your money. By prioritizing needs over wants, avoiding impulse buys, and taking advantage of discounts, you can get the most out of your money. Delayed gratification and budgeting for fun help you enjoy your money responsibly while still working towards your financial goals. In the next chapter, we'll explore the concepts of credit and debt, and how to manage them wisely.

Chapter 7: Understanding Credit and Debt

What is Credit?

Credit is the ability to borrow money with the promise to repay it later, often with interest. It's a powerful financial tool that can help you make significant purchases and build a positive financial reputation when used wisely.

The Importance of Credit

Good credit is essential because it affects your ability to:

- **Borrow Money:** Get loans for large purchases like a car or house.
- **Get Better Interest Rates:** Lower interest rates save you money over time.
- **Rent an Apartment:** Landlords often check credit scores.
- **Get a Job:** Some employers check credit history as part of the hiring process.

Types of Credit

1. Revolving Credit: This includes credit cards where you can borrow up to a certain limit and repay it over time. You can continue borrowing as long as you don't exceed the limit.
2. Installment Credit: This includes loans where you borrow a specific amount and repay it in fixed monthly payments over a set period, such as student loans or car loans.

What is a Credit Score?

A credit score is a number that represents your creditworthiness. It's based on your credit history, which includes how much debt you have, your repayment history, and other factors. Scores range from 300 to 850, with higher scores indicating better creditworthiness.

How to Build Good Credit

1. Pay Bills on Time: Always pay your bills by the due date. Late payments can significantly harm your credit score.
2. Keep Balances Low: Avoid maxing out your credit cards. Try to keep your balance below 30% of your credit limit.
3. Don't Open Too Many Accounts: Each credit application can slightly lower your credit score. Only apply for credit when necessary.
4. Monitor Your Credit Report: Regularly check your credit report for errors and dispute any inaccuracies.

The Risks of Credit

While credit can be beneficial, it comes with risks:

- **High-Interest Rates:** If you don't pay off your balance each month, interest can accumulate quickly.
- **Debt Accumulation:** It's easy to fall into the trap of overspending and accumulating debt.
- **Negative Impact on Credit Score:** Mismanaging credit can lower your credit score, making it harder to borrow in the future.

Understanding Debt

Debt is money you owe to others. It can be a useful tool when managed responsibly but can become overwhelming if not handled properly.

Types of Debt

1. Secured Debt: This debt is backed by collateral, such as a mortgage (backed by your house) or a car loan (backed by your car). If you don't repay, the lender can take the collateral.

2. Unsecured Debt: This debt is not backed by collateral, such as credit card debt or medical bills. If you don't repay, the lender can take legal action to recover the debt.

Managing Debt Wisely

1. Create a Repayment Plan: List all your debts and create a plan to repay them. Focus on paying off high-interest debt first.

2. Avoid Taking on More Debt: Only borrow what you can afford to repay. Avoid using credit for unnecessary purchases.

3. Consider Debt Consolidation: If you have multiple debts, consolidating them into a single loan with a lower interest rate can simplify repayment and save you money.

4. Seek Help if Needed: If you're struggling with debt, seek advice from a financial advisor or credit counselor.

The Impact of Debt on Your Future

Excessive debt can limit your financial freedom and affect your ability to achieve long-term goals. It can lead to stress, impact your credit score, and reduce your ability to save and invest for the future.

Activity: Create a Credit and Debt Plan

1. List Your Credit Accounts: Write down all your credit accounts, including credit cards, loans, and any other forms of credit.
2. Track Your Debt: Note the balance, interest rate, and minimum payment for each debt.
3. Plan Your Payments: Create a plan to pay off your debts, focusing on high-interest accounts first.
4. Monitor Your Progress: Regularly review your credit and debt plan to ensure you're on track.

Summary

Understanding credit and debt is essential for managing your finances responsibly. Good credit opens doors to financial opportunities, while managing debt wisely prevents financial stress. By building good credit habits and being mindful of your borrowing, you can use credit to your advantage while avoiding the pitfalls of debt. In the next chapter, we'll explore the basics of investing and how to start growing your wealth.

Chapter 8: Introduction to Investing

What is Investing?

Investing is the process of putting money into financial assets with the expectation of generating a profit over time. Unlike saving, which focuses on preserving money, investing aims to grow your wealth by taking advantage of the potential for higher returns.

Why Invest?

Investing is important for several reasons:

- **Grow Your Wealth:** Investing can help your money grow faster than it would in a savings account.
- **Beat Inflation:** Inflation reduces the purchasing power of money over time. Investing can help you stay ahead of inflation.
- **Achieve Financial Goals:** Investing can help you reach long-term financial goals like buying a house, funding education, or retiring comfortably.
- **Passive Income:** Investments can provide passive income through dividends, interest, or capital gains.

The Basics of Investing

Before you start investing, it's essential to understand some key concepts:

1. Risk and Return

- **Risk:** The potential for losing some or all of your investment. Different investments carry different levels of risk.
- **Return:** The profit you earn from your investment. Generally, higher risk investments offer the potential for higher returns.

2. Diversification

Diversification is spreading your investments across different types of assets to reduce risk. By not putting all your money into one investment, you lower the chance of losing everything if one investment performs poorly.

3. Compound Interest

Compound interest is earning interest on both the money you've invested and the interest that money earns. Over time, this can significantly increase your investment returns.

Types of Investments

Here are some common types of investments:

1. Stocks

Stocks represent ownership in a company. When you buy a stock, you become a shareholder and own a part of that company. Stocks can provide high returns but also come with higher risk.

2. Bonds

Bonds are loans you make to a company or government in exchange for periodic interest payments and the return of the bond's face value when it matures. Bonds are generally less risky than stocks but offer lower returns.

3. Mutual Funds

Mutual funds pool money from many investors to buy a diversified portfolio of stocks, bonds, or other securities. This allows you to invest in a variety of assets without having to buy each one individually.

4. Exchange-Traded Funds (ETFs)

ETFs are similar to mutual funds but trade like stocks on an exchange. They offer diversification and can be bought and sold throughout the trading day at market prices.

5. Real Estate

Investing in real estate involves buying property to generate rental income or sell at a higher price in the future. Real estate can provide steady income and potential appreciation but requires significant capital and management.

How to Start Investing

1. Educate Yourself

Learn as much as you can about investing. Read books, take online courses, and follow financial news to understand how different investments work and the risks involved.

2. Set Financial Goals

Determine what you want to achieve with your investments. Setting clear goals helps you choose the right investments and stay focused.

3. Start Small

You don't need a lot of money to start investing. Many platforms allow you to start with small amounts. The key is to start early and consistently invest over time.

4. Choose an Investment Account

Open an investment account that suits your needs. Common options include:

- **Brokerage Accounts:** Allow you to buy and sell a wide range of investments.
- **Robo-Advisors:** Provide automated, algorithm-driven financial planning services with minimal human supervision.
- **Retirement Accounts:** Such as IRAs or 401(k)s, offer tax advantages for long-term savings.

5. Diversify Your Portfolio

Spread your investments across different asset classes to reduce risk. A diversified portfolio can help protect you against losses in any single investment.

6. Monitor and Adjust

Regularly review your investments to ensure they align with your goals and risk tolerance. Make adjustments as needed based on market conditions and changes in your financial situation.

The Power of Starting Early

The earlier you start investing, the more you can benefit from compound interest. Even small investments can grow significantly over time, so don't wait to start building your investment portfolio.

Activity: Create a Mock Investment Portfolio

To practice investing, create a mock investment portfolio:

1. **Set a Budget:** Decide how much imaginary money you have to invest.
2. **Choose Investments:** Select a mix of stocks, bonds, mutual funds, and ETFs.
3. **Track Performance:** Monitor your portfolio over a few months to see how it performs. Use online tools or apps to simulate real market conditions.

Summary

Investing is a powerful way to grow your wealth and achieve your financial goals. By understanding the basics of risk and return, diversification, and compound interest, you can make informed investment decisions. Start small, educate yourself, and take advantage of the benefits of investing early. In the next chapter, we'll discuss how to set and achieve financial goals, helping you create a roadmap for your financial future.

Chapter 9: Setting and Achieving Financial Goals

Why Set Financial Goals?

Setting financial goals is crucial for managing your money effectively and achieving your dreams. Goals provide direction, motivation, and a clear plan for how to use your money. Whether it's saving for college, buying a car, or going on a vacation, financial goals help you stay focused and disciplined.

Types of Financial Goals

Financial goals can be short-term, medium-term, or long-term, depending on how soon you want to achieve them.

1. Short-Term Goals

These are goals you want to achieve within the next year. Examples include:

- Saving for a new gadget
- Building an emergency fund
- Paying off a small debt

2. Medium-Term Goals

These are goals you aim to achieve in one to five years. Examples include:

- Saving for a car
- Building a college fund
- Taking a significant vacation

3. Long-Term Goals

These are goals that take more than five years to achieve. Examples include:

- Saving for higher education
- Buying a house
- Retirement planning

How to Set Financial Goals

Setting financial goals involves a few key steps to ensure they are clear and achievable.

1. Be Specific

Clearly define what you want to achieve. Instead of saying, "I want to save money," specify, "I want to save $1,000 for a new laptop."

2. Make Them Measurable

Ensure you can track your progress. For example, "I will save $100 per month for ten months to reach my goal of $1,000."

3. Set Realistic Goals

Make sure your goals are achievable given your current financial situation. Setting unattainable goals can lead to frustration and loss of motivation.

4. Set a Time Frame

Give yourself a deadline to achieve your goals. Having a time frame creates a sense of urgency and helps you stay on track.

5. Break Them Down

Divide larger goals into smaller, manageable steps. For example, if your goal is to save $1,200 in a year, break it down to saving $100 each month.

Creating a Financial Goals Plan

Once you've set your goals, create a plan to achieve them. Here's how:

1. List Your Goals

Write down all your financial goals, categorizing them as short-term, medium-term, or long-term.

2. Prioritize Your Goals

Determine which goals are most important to you and focus on those first. Consider your needs and wants when prioritizing.

3. Calculate the Cost

Figure out how much money you need for each goal. This helps you understand what you need to save and budget accordingly.

4. Create a Savings Plan

Decide how much money you need to save each week or month to reach your goals. Automate your savings if possible to ensure consistency.

5. Track Your Progress

Regularly review your progress towards your goals. Adjust your plan as needed to stay on track.

Tools for Achieving Financial Goals

Utilize tools and resources to help you manage and track your financial goals:

1. Budgeting Apps

Apps like Mint, YNAB (You Need a Budget), and PocketGuard can help you create and stick to a budget, making it easier to save for your goals.

2. Savings Accounts

Open a separate savings account for each of your major goals. This keeps your savings organized and prevents you from accidentally spending the money.

3. Goal-Tracking Sheets

Use goal-tracking sheets or digital spreadsheets to visually track your progress. Seeing your progress can be motivating and help you stay focused.

Activity: Create Your Financial Goals Plan

1. Identify Your Goals: Write down at least three financial goals, specifying whether they are short-term, medium-term, or long-term.
2. Detail Your Plan: For each goal, determine how much you need to save, your time frame, and your monthly savings target.
3. Set Up Tracking: Create a tracking sheet or use an app to monitor your progress.
4. Review Regularly: Set a reminder to review your goals and progress each month.

Staying Motivated

Achieving financial goals requires discipline and motivation. Here are some tips to stay motivated:

- **Celebrate Milestones:** Reward yourself when you reach milestones on your way to your larger goals.
- **Visualize Success:** Imagine how achieving your goals will feel and the benefits it will bring.
- **Stay Positive:** Focus on your progress and stay positive, even if setbacks occur.

Summary

Setting and achieving financial goals is a vital part of managing your money effectively. By being specific, measurable, realistic, and timely with your goals, and by creating a clear plan to achieve them, you can make your financial dreams a reality. Use tools like budgeting apps and savings accounts to stay organized and track your progress.

Chapter 10: Earning Money

Why Earning Money Matters?

Earning money is a fundamental part of financial independence and personal growth. Whether it's through a part-time job, freelancing, or starting your own business, earning money allows you to support yourself, save for the future, and pursue your goals and interests.

Types of Income

Income can come in various forms, including:

1. Earned Income

Earned income is money you receive in exchange for work or services you provide. This includes:

- **Wages and Salaries:** Payment from an employer for work done.
- **Tips and Bonuses:** Additional compensation for good performance or exceptional service.
- **Commissions:** Earnings based on sales or performance targets.
- **Self-Employment Income:** Money earned from running your own business or freelancing.

2. Passive Income

Passive income is money you earn with little to no ongoing effort. Examples include:

- **Rental Income:** Money earned from renting out property you own.
- **Dividend Income:** Payments received from owning stocks or shares in companies.
- **Interest Income:** Money earned from interest on savings accounts, bonds, or other investments.

3. Portfolio Income

Portfolio income is money generated from investments. This includes:

Capital Gains: Profit earned from selling investments like stocks, real estate, or collectibles.
Interest and Dividends: Income earned from interest payments on bonds or dividends from stocks.

How to Earn Money

There are various ways to earn money as a teenager:

1. Part-Time Jobs

Working a part-time job is a common way for teenagers to earn money. Look for opportunities at local businesses, restaurants, retail stores, or through online platforms.

2. Freelancing

If you have skills like writing, graphic design, or coding, you can offer your services as a freelancer. Websites like Upwork, Fiverr, and Freelancer connect freelancers with clients seeking their expertise.

3. Starting a Business

If you have an entrepreneurial spirit, consider starting your own business. This could be anything from selling handmade crafts online to offering tutoring services in your community.

4. Babysitting or Pet Sitting

Providing childcare or pet sitting services can be a lucrative way to earn money, especially if you enjoy working with children or animals.

Tips for Earning Money

1. Explore Your Interests

Look for opportunities that align with your interests and skills. Enjoying what you do makes work more enjoyable and increases your chances of success.

2. Be Proactive

Don't wait for opportunities to come to you. Take initiative by reaching out to potential employers, clients, or customers.

3. Network

Networking is essential for finding job opportunities and building relationships with potential clients. Attend career fairs, join professional organizations, and connect with people in your desired field.

4. Manage Your Time Wisely

Balancing work, school, and other commitments requires effective time management. Prioritize tasks, set realistic goals, and avoid procrastination to make the most of your time.

5. Save and Budget

Develop good money management habits by saving a portion of your earnings and budgeting for expenses. This helps you build financial security and avoid overspending.

Activity: Explore Income Opportunities

1. Identify Your Interests and Skills: Make a list of activities you enjoy and skills you possess.
2. Research Opportunities: Explore job listings, freelancing platforms, and local businesses to find opportunities that match your interests and skills.
3. Set Goals: Define your financial goals and how much money you want to earn. Break down your goals into actionable steps to achieve them.
4. Take Action: Apply for jobs, create a freelancing profile, or start planning your business idea. Don't be afraid to take the first step towards earning money.

Summary

Earning money is a valuable skill that provides financial independence and opens up opportunities for personal and professional growth. Whether through part-time jobs, freelancing, or entrepreneurship, there are various ways for teenagers to earn money and gain valuable experience. By exploring your interests, being proactive, and managing your time and finances effectively, you can successfully earn money while pursuing your goals and aspirations. In the next chapter, we'll discuss the basics of taxes and how they impact your finances.

Chapter 11: Understanding Taxes

What Are Taxes?

Taxes are mandatory contributions that individuals and businesses pay to the government. These funds are used to provide public services and infrastructure, such as schools, roads, and healthcare. Understanding taxes is crucial for managing your finances and ensuring you comply with legal requirements.

Why Do We Pay Taxes?

Taxes are essential for the functioning of society. They help fund:

- **Public Services:** Education, healthcare, and emergency services.
- **Infrastructure:** Roads, bridges, public transportation.
- **Government Operations:** Salaries for government employees, maintenance of public buildings.
- **Social Programs:** Welfare, unemployment benefits, Social Security.

Types of Taxes

There are several types of taxes that you may encounter:

1. Income Tax

Income tax is a percentage of your earnings that you pay to the federal, state, and sometimes local governments. It is based on your income level and is usually withheld from your paycheck by your employer.

2. Sales Tax

Sales tax is a tax on goods and services you purchase. The rate varies by state and locality. This tax is added to the price of items you buy at the store.

3. Property Tax

Property tax is a tax on property you own, such as a house or land. This tax is usually paid annually to local governments and is based on the property's value.

4. Payroll Tax

Payroll taxes are taxes withheld from your paycheck by your employer. These include Social Security and Medicare taxes, which fund retirement and healthcare programs for the elderly and disabled.

5. Capital Gains Tax

Capital gains tax is a tax on the profit you make from selling investments like stocks or real estate. The rate depends on how long you held the investment and your income level.

How Income Tax Works

Understanding how income tax works can help you manage your finances and file your tax return correctly.

1. Tax Brackets

The U.S. federal income tax system is progressive, meaning that the tax rate increases as your income increases. Tax brackets are the ranges of income that are taxed at different rates. Here's an example of how tax brackets work:

- **10%:** $0 to $9,875
- **12%:** $9,876 to $40,125
- **22%:** $40,126 to $85,525
- **24%:** $85,526 to $163,300
- **32%:** $163,301 to $207,350
- **35%:** $207,351 to $518,400
- **37%:** Over $518,400

2. Filing Status

Your filing status determines the tax rates and standard deductions that apply to you. Common statuses include:

- **Single:** Unmarried individuals.
- **Married Filing Jointly:** Married couples filing together.
- **Married Filing Separately:** Married couples filing separately.
- **Head of Household:** Unmarried individuals with dependents.

3. Deductions and Credits

Deductions and credits can reduce your taxable income and the amount of tax you owe:

- **Standard Deduction:** A fixed amount you can subtract from your income.
- **Itemized Deductions:** Specific expenses like medical costs or mortgage interest that you can subtract from your income.
- **Tax Credits:** Direct reductions in the amount of tax you owe, such as the Earned Income Tax Credit (EITC).

How to File Taxes

Filing your taxes involves several steps:

1. Gather Documents

Collect all necessary documents, including:

- **W-2 Forms:** Report income and taxes withheld by your employer.
- **1099 Forms:** Report other types of income like freelance work.
- **Receipts:** For deductible expenses like charitable donations.

2. Choose a Filing Method

Decide how you want to file your taxes:

- **Manual Filing:** Fill out paper forms and mail them to the IRS.
- **Tax Software:** Use software like TurboTax or H&R Block to file online.
- **Professional Help:** Hire a tax professional to prepare and file your return.

3. Complete Your Tax Return

Follow the instructions to complete your tax return, entering your income, deductions, and credits. The software or tax professional will help calculate how much tax you owe or the refund you're due.

4. Submit Your Return

File your tax return by the deadline, usually April 15th. If you owe taxes, pay them by this date to avoid penalties and interest.

Understanding Your Paycheck

Your paycheck provides important information about your income and taxes:

- **Gross Pay:** Your total earnings before taxes and deductions.
- **Net Pay:** Your take-home pay after taxes and deductions.
- Withholdings: Amounts withheld for federal and state taxes, Social Security, and Medicare.
- **Deductions:** Other amounts taken from your paycheck, like health insurance premiums or retirement contributions.

Activity: Understanding a Pay Stub

1. Obtain a Sample Pay Stub: Find a sample pay stub online or use a real one if you have a part-time job.
2. Identify Key Components: Identify gross pay, net pay, withholdings, and deductions.
3. Calculate Take-Home Pay: Practice calculating your net pay by subtracting withholdings and deductions from gross pay.

Summary

Understanding taxes is essential for managing your finances responsibly. Taxes fund vital public services and infrastructure, and knowing how to file your tax return ensures you comply with the law and take advantage of deductions and credits. By learning about different types of taxes, how income tax works, and how to read your paycheck, you can make informed financial decisions.

Chapter 12: Protecting Your Finances

Why Protecting Your Finances Is Important

Protecting your finances is essential for safeguarding your hard-earned money and ensuring financial security. By taking proactive steps to protect yourself against potential risks and threats, you can minimize financial losses and maintain control over your financial future.

Common Financial Risks

1. Identity Theft

Identity theft occurs when someone steals your personal information, such as your Social Security number or credit card details, to commit fraud or other crimes.

2. Fraudulent Transactions

Fraudulent transactions involve unauthorized charges or purchases made using your credit card, bank account, or other financial accounts.

3. Scams

Scams are deceptive schemes designed to trick individuals into giving away their money or personal information. Common scams include phishing emails, fake job offers, and lottery scams.

Tips for Protecting Your Finances

1. Safeguard Personal Information

- **Keep Your Social Security Number Secure:** Avoid carrying your Social Security card with you and only provide it when necessary.
- **Protect Your Online Accounts:** Use strong, unique passwords for your online accounts and enable two-factor authentication when available.
- **Be Wary of Sharing Information:** Avoid sharing sensitive information like your bank account or credit card details with unknown or unverified individuals or websites.

2. Monitor Your Accounts Regularly

- **Review Your Bank Statements:** Check your bank and credit card statements regularly for any unauthorized transactions.
- **Monitor Your Credit Report:** Request a free credit report annually from each of the three major credit bureaus (Equifax, Experian, TransUnion) and review it for any inaccuracies or signs of identity theft.

3. Be Skeptical of Unsolicited Offers

- **Don't Click on Suspicious Links:** Avoid clicking on links or downloading attachments from unsolicited emails or text messages, especially if they seem suspicious or too good to be true.
- **Verify Caller Identities:** Be cautious when providing personal information over the phone, and verify the identity of the caller before sharing any sensitive information.

4. Secure Your Devices and Networks

- **Use Antivirus Software:** Install reputable antivirus software on your computer and mobile devices to protect against malware and other cyber threats.
- **Secure Your Wi-Fi Network:** Use strong passwords and encryption protocols to secure your home Wi-Fi network and prevent unauthorized access.

Responding to Financial Fraud or Identity Theft

1. Report Unauthorized Transactions

- **Contact Your Financial Institution:** Notify your bank or credit card issuer immediately if you notice any unauthorized transactions on your accounts.
- **File a Police Report:** File a report with your local police department to document the fraud and protect yourself from further liability.

2. Place a Fraud Alert or Credit Freeze

- **Fraud Alert:** Contact one of the three major credit bureaus to place a fraud alert on your credit report, which notifies lenders to take extra steps to verify your identity before extending credit.
- **Credit Freeze:** Consider placing a credit freeze on your credit report to restrict access to your credit information and prevent new accounts from being opened in your name.

3. Monitor Your Accounts Closely

- **Continue Monitoring:** Keep a close eye on your financial accounts and credit report for any signs of suspicious activity, even after taking initial steps to address the fraud.

Activity: Protect Your Personal Information

1. Review Your Security Practices: Assess your current habits and practices for safeguarding your personal information.
2. Update Your Passwords: Change passwords for your online accounts to stronger, more secure ones.
3. Enable Two-Factor Authentication: Activate two-factor authentication for your most important online accounts for an extra layer of security.
4. Educate Yourself: Research common scams and fraud schemes to learn how to recognize and avoid them.

Summary

Protecting your finances is crucial for maintaining financial security and peace of mind. By taking proactive steps to safeguard your personal information, monitor your accounts regularly, and respond promptly to any signs of fraud or identity theft, you can minimize the risk of financial losses and protect yourself against potential threats. Stay vigilant, stay informed, and prioritize the security of your finances to ensure a bright financial future.

Chapter 13: Financial Tools and Resources

Introduction to Financial Tools

Financial tools and resources are essential for managing your money effectively, making informed financial decisions, and achieving your financial goals. Whether you're budgeting, saving, investing, or planning for the future, there are various tools and resources available to help you navigate the world of personal finance.

Budgeting Tools

1. Budgeting Apps

Budgeting apps like Mint, YNAB (You Need a Budget), and PocketGuard help you track your spending, set savings goals, and create budgets tailored to your financial situation.

2. Spreadsheet Templates

Excel or Google Sheets offer customizable spreadsheet templates for budgeting, allowing you to organize your income, expenses, and savings goals in a format that works for you.

Saving and Investing Tools

1. Savings Accounts

Online savings accounts like Ally Bank or Marcus by Goldman Sachs offer competitive interest rates and easy access to your money, making them ideal for short-term savings goals.

2. Investment Apps

Investment apps like Robinhood, Acorns, and Stash allow you to start investing with small amounts of money, offering features like commission-free trading, automated portfolio management, and educational resources.

Retirement Planning Tools

1. Retirement Calculators

Retirement calculators like the one offered by Vanguard or Fidelity help you estimate how much money you'll need to retire comfortably and create a plan to reach your retirement goals.

2. Retirement Accounts

Retirement accounts like IRAs (Individual Retirement Accounts) and 401(k)s offer tax advantages and investment options to help you save for retirement, whether through employer-sponsored plans or individual accounts.

Credit and Debt Management Tools

1. Credit Monitoring Services

Credit monitoring services like Credit Karma or Experian allow you to track changes to your credit report, monitor your credit score, and receive alerts about potential identity theft or fraud.

2. Debt Repayment Calculators

Debt repayment calculators help you create a plan to pay off debt faster by calculating how much you need to pay each month to eliminate debt by a certain date and save on interest.

Financial Education Resources

1. Books and Publications

Books like **"The Total Money Makeover"** by **Dave Ramsey**, **"Rich Dad Poor Dad"** by **Robert Kiyosaki**, and **"I Will Teach You to Be Rich"** by **Ramit Sethi** offer valuable insights and strategies for managing money, building wealth, and achieving financial independence.

2. Online Courses and Webinars

Online courses and webinars from platforms like Coursera, Udemy, and Khan Academy provide accessible and affordable education on a wide range of financial topics, including budgeting, investing, and retirement planning.

Government Resources

1. Financial Aid and Student Loans

Government websites like StudentAid.gov offer information and resources on financial aid programs, scholarships, grants, and student loans to help you finance your education.

2. Consumer Protection Agencies

Consumer protection agencies like the Consumer Financial Protection Bureau (CFPB) provide resources and tools to help consumers understand their rights, make informed financial decisions, and protect themselves against fraud and abuse.

Summary

Financial tools and resources are invaluable assets for managing your money, achieving your financial goals, and building a secure financial future. Whether you're budgeting, saving, investing, or planning for retirement, there are tools available to help you every step of the way. By leveraging these tools and resources, educating yourself about personal finance, and taking control of your financial life, you can make smart decisions that lead to long-term financial success. In the next chapter, we'll explore the concept of giving back and the importance of philanthropy in your financial journey.

Chapter 14: The Importance of Philanthropy

Understanding Philanthropy

Philanthropy, often associated with charitable giving and generosity, plays a significant role in society by addressing social issues, supporting communities, and making a positive impact on the world. As a teenager, you may wonder why philanthropy matters and how you can get involved. Let's explore the importance of philanthropy and how it can benefit both individuals and society as a whole.

Building Empathy and Compassion

Engaging in philanthropic activities, such as volunteering or donating to charitable causes, fosters empathy and compassion towards others. By witnessing the struggles and challenges faced by individuals and communities in need, you develop a greater understanding of the world around you and the power of kindness and generosity.

Creating Positive Change

Philanthropy has the power to create positive change and address pressing social issues, such as poverty, homelessness, education inequality, and environmental conservation. Through charitable giving and community involvement, individuals and organizations can contribute to solutions that improve the lives of others and create a more equitable and sustainable society.

Fostering Social Responsibility

Participating in philanthropic initiatives promotes social responsibility and civic engagement among individuals, businesses, and communities. By taking an active role in addressing social challenges and giving back to those in need, you become an agent of change and contribute to the collective well-being of society.

Empowering Communities

Philanthropy empowers communities by providing resources, support, and opportunities for growth and development. Whether through funding for education programs, healthcare services, or economic development initiatives, philanthropic efforts help communities thrive and build a brighter future for all members.

Cultivating Gratitude and Fulfillment

Practicing philanthropy cultivates gratitude and fulfillment by giving you the opportunity to make a positive impact on the lives of others. The act of giving back not only benefits those in need but also brings joy, satisfaction, and a sense of purpose to the giver, enhancing overall well-being and happiness.

Inspiring Others

Your involvement in philanthropy can inspire and motivate others to take action and make a difference in their own communities. By leading by example and sharing your experiences and passion for giving back, you encourage others to join you in creating positive change and building a better world for future generations.

Getting Involved in Philanthropy

There are many ways for teenagers to get involved in philanthropy and make a difference in their communities:

- **Volunteer:** Find local organizations or causes that align with your interests and donate your time and skills to support their efforts.
- **Donate:** Consider donating money, goods, or resources to charitable organizations or fundraising campaigns that are making an impact in areas you care about.
- **Raise Awareness:** Use your voice and platform to raise awareness about important social issues and advocate for positive change in your community and beyond.
- **Start a Project:** Initiate a philanthropic project or campaign to address a specific need or issue in your community, such as organizing a food drive, fundraiser, or community clean-up event.

Summary

Philanthropy is not just about giving money—it's about making a meaningful difference in the lives of others and contributing to the greater good of society. As a teenager, you have the power to create positive change and leave a lasting impact on your community and the world. By embracing the values of empathy, compassion, and social responsibility, and taking action to support causes you believe in, you can become a force for good and help build a brighter future for all.

Conclusion

Congratulations on completing **"Money Matters: A Teen's Guide to Financial Education"**! By exploring the essential concepts of personal finance, from budgeting and saving to investing and protecting your finances, you've taken an important step towards building a solid foundation for your financial future.

As a teenager, you have a unique opportunity to develop good money habits early on, setting yourself up for success as you transition into adulthood. By applying the knowledge and skills you've gained from this book, you can take control of your finances, make informed decisions, and work towards achieving your financial goals.

Remember, financial education is a lifelong journey. Stay curious, continue learning, and don't be afraid to seek guidance when needed. Whether it's from books, online resources, or trusted mentors, there are plenty of resources available to support you on your financial journey.

As you embark on this journey, always keep your values and priorities in mind. Money is a tool that can help you achieve your goals and dreams, but true wealth is about more than just dollars and cents. Cultivate relationships, pursue passions, and strive for a balanced life that brings you happiness and fulfillment.

Finally, don't forget the importance of giving back. As you build wealth and achieve success, consider how you can use your resources to make a positive impact on others and contribute to the well-being of your community and the world.

Thank you for joining us on this journey through **"Money Matters: A Teen's Guide to Financial Education."** We wish you all the best as you navigate the exciting world of personal finance and work towards a brighter financial future. Remember, the power to shape your financial destiny is in your hands. Go forth with confidence and make your money matter!

Glossary

Budget: A plan for managing your money, outlining your income and expenses to ensure you're spending within your means and saving for your goals.

Compound Interest: Interest that's calculated on both the initial principal and the accumulated interest of previous periods, resulting in exponential growth of your savings or investments over time.

Credit Score: A numerical representation of your creditworthiness, based on your credit history, payment behavior, and other financial factors. Lenders use credit scores to assess the risk of lending you money.

Diversification: Spreading your investments across different assets to reduce risk. By diversifying, you minimize the impact of poor performance in any single investment.

Financial Goals: Specific objectives you set for your financial future, such as saving for a house, paying off debt, or building an emergency fund.

Income Tax: A tax on your earnings, imposed by federal, state, and sometimes local governments. The amount you owe is based on your income level and filing status.

Investment: Putting money into financial assets with the expectation of generating a profit over time. Common investments include stocks, bonds, mutual funds, and real estate.

Net Worth: The difference between your assets (what you own) and your liabilities (what you owe). It's a measure of your overall financial health and wealth.

Passive Income: Money earned with little to no ongoing effort. Examples include rental income, dividends from stocks, and interest from savings accounts.

Portfolio: A collection of investments owned by an individual or institution, such as stocks, bonds, mutual funds, and ETFs.

Risk: The potential for financial loss or uncertainty in the outcome of an investment. Generally, higher-risk investments offer the potential for higher returns.

Savings Account: A bank account that allows you to deposit money and earn interest on your savings. Savings accounts offer liquidity and safety for short-term financial goals.

Stocks: Securities that represent ownership in a company. When you buy stock, you become a shareholder and own a portion of the company's assets and earnings.

Tax Deduction: An expense that you can subtract from your taxable income, reducing the amount of tax you owe. Common deductions include mortgage interest, charitable contributions, and student loan interest.

Tax Withholding: The amount of money your employer deducts from your paycheck to cover your income tax liability. Withholding is based on your income, filing status, and the number of allowances you claim on your W-4 form.

Two-Factor Authentication (2FA): A security process that requires users to provide two different forms of identification before accessing an online account. This typically involves something you know (like a password) and something you have (like a code sent to your phone).

Wealth: The abundance of valuable resources or assets, including money, property, and investments. True wealth encompasses financial stability, security, and the ability to achieve your goals and dreams.

Resources for Further Learning

Books

1. "The Total Money Makeover" by Dave Ramsey: Offers practical advice on budgeting, saving, and getting out of debt.

2. "Rich Dad Poor Dad" by Robert Kiyosaki: Explores the differences in mindset and financial strategies between the author's "rich" dad and "poor" dad.

3. "I Will Teach You to Be Rich" by Ramit Sethi: Provides step-by-step instructions for managing money, investing, and building wealth.

Online Courses

1. Coursera: Offers a wide range of courses on personal finance, investing, and financial planning from top universities and institutions.

2. Udemy: Provides affordable courses on budgeting, investing, and financial literacy taught by experts in the field.

3. Khan Academy: Offers free, self-paced courses on economics and finance topics, including banking, taxes, and investing.

Websites

1. Investopedia: A comprehensive resource for learning about investing, financial markets, and economics, with articles, tutorials, and investing guides.

2. NerdWallet: Provides information and tools for managing your finances, including budgeting calculators, credit card reviews, and investment guides.

3. The Balance: Offers expert advice and resources on personal finance topics like budgeting, saving, and investing, as well as career and small business advice.

Podcasts

1. The Dave Ramsey Show: Hosted by personal finance expert Dave Ramsey, this podcast offers practical advice on getting out of debt, saving money, and building wealth.

2. So Money with Farnoosh Torabi: Features interviews with entrepreneurs, authors, and financial experts discussing money management, investing, and career success.

3. The Investing for Beginners Podcast: Provides beginner-friendly advice and insights on investing in stocks, bonds, and other assets.

Government Resources

1. StudentAid.gov: Offers information and resources on federal student aid programs, scholarships, grants, and student loans to help finance your education.

2. MyMoney.gov: Provides tools and resources for managing your finances, understanding credit, and planning for the future, sponsored by the U.S. government.

3. IRS.gov: Offers tax information, forms, and resources to help you understand your tax obligations and file your tax return accurately and on time.

Financial Apps

1. Mint: A budgeting app that helps you track your spending, set savings goals, and manage your finances in one place.

2. Acorns: An investment app that rounds up your everyday purchases to the nearest dollar and invests the spare change in a diversified portfolio.

3. Robinhood: A commission-free investing app that allows you to buy and sell stocks, ETFs, and cryptocurrencies with no trading fees.

Social Media

1. YouTube: Offers a wealth of personal finance channels and content creators sharing tips, advice, and insights on budgeting, saving, and investing.

2. Instagram: Follow personal finance influencers and accounts for daily tips, motivation, and inspiration to help you achieve your financial goals.

3. Reddit: Join personal finance communities like r/personalfinance and r/investing for advice, discussions, and answers to your financial questions.

Local Resources

1. Public Libraries: Visit your local library for books, workshops, and resources on personal finance and money management.

2. Community Centers: Check out community centers or nonprofit organizations in your area for workshops, classes, and events focused on financial literacy and education.

3. Financial Institutions: Contact local banks or credit unions to inquire about financial literacy programs, seminars, or resources available to customers and the community.

Summary

These resources offer valuable information and tools to help you continue your journey towards financial literacy and independence. Remember, lifelong learning is key to achieving your financial goals and building a secure future. Explore these resources, ask questions, and empower yourself with knowledge to make informed financial decisions. Your financial future is in your hands—take control and make it count!

Podcasts

1. The Dave Ramsey Show: Hosted by personal finance expert Dave Ramsey, this podcast offers practical advice on getting out of debt, saving money, and building wealth.

2. So Money with Farnoosh Torabi: Features interviews with entrepreneurs, authors, and financial experts discussing money management, investing, and career success.

3. The Investing for Beginners Podcast: Provides beginner-friendly advice and insights on investing in stocks, bonds, and other assets.

Government Resources

1. StudentAid.gov: Offers information and resources on federal student aid programs, scholarships, grants, and student loans to help finance your education.

2. MyMoney.gov: Provides tools and resources for managing your finances, understanding credit, and planning for the future, sponsored by the U.S. government.

3. IRS.gov: Offers tax information, forms, and resources to help you understand your tax obligations and file your tax return accurately and on time.

Financial Apps

1. Mint: A budgeting app that helps you track your spending, set savings goals, and manage your finances in one place.

2. Acorns: An investment app that rounds up your everyday purchases to the nearest dollar and invests the spare change in a diversified portfolio.

3. Robinhood: A commission-free investing app that allows you to buy and sell stocks, ETFs, and cryptocurrencies with no trading fees.

Social Media

1. YouTube: Offers a wealth of personal finance channels and content creators sharing tips, advice, and insights on budgeting, saving, and investing.

2. Instagram: Follow personal finance influencers and accounts for daily tips, motivation, and inspiration to help you achieve your financial goals.

3. Reddit: Join personal finance communities like r/personalfinance and r/investing for advice, discussions, and answers to your financial questions.

Local Resources

1. Public Libraries: Visit your local library for books, workshops, and resources on personal finance and money management.

2. Community Centers: Check out community centers or nonprofit organizations in your area for workshops, classes, and events focused on financial literacy and education.

3. Financial Institutions: Contact local banks or credit unions to inquire about financial literacy programs, seminars, or resources available to customers and the community.

Summary

These resources offer valuable information and tools to help you continue your journey towards financial literacy and independence. Remember, lifelong learning is key to achieving your financial goals and building a secure future. Explore these resources, ask questions, and empower yourself with knowledge to make informed financial decisions. Your financial future is in your hands—take control and make it count!

Disclaimer:

The content of this book, **"Money Matters: A Teen's Guide to Financial Education,"** has been generated with the assistance of artificial intelligence (AI) technology. While the information provided is based on common financial knowledge and practices as of the time of its creation, it may not be exhaustive or fully up-to-date with the latest developments in the field of personal finance.

Readers are encouraged to supplement the information provided in this book with additional research and advice from qualified financial professionals. The authors and publishers of this book have made every effort to ensure accuracy, completeness, or applicability of the information presented herein.

Furthermore, the content of this book is intended for educational purposes only and should not be construed as financial, legal, or investment advice. Each individual's financial situation is unique, and readers are advised to consult with a qualified financial advisor or professional before making any financial decisions or taking any actions based on the information contained in this book.

By reading this book, you acknowledge and agree that the authors, publishers, and contributors are not liable for any losses, damages, or consequences arising from the use or misuse of the information provided herein.

www.ingramcontent.com/pod-product-compliance
Lightning Source LLC
Chambersburg PA
CBHW062316220526
45479CB00004B/1191